WAYFARER

RE-IMAGINING THE POSSIBLE ✱ CHARTING THE WAY FOR CHANGE

"True resistance begins with people confronting pain…and wanting to do something to change it."

—BELL HOOKS

Since 2012, *The Wayfarer* has been offering literature, interviews, and art with the intention to inspire our readers and highlight the power for agency and change-making that each individual holds.

By our definition, a "wayfarer" is one whose inner compass is ever-oriented to truth, wisdom, healing, and beauty in their own wandering.

The Wayfarer's mission as a publication is to foster a community of contemplative voices and provide readers with resources and perspectives that support them in their own journey.

As we move into our 10th year, in the face of these uncertain times, we renew our commitment to our readers to be a space of solace and our pledge to advocate for marginalized communities, the arts, and environmental conservation.

A LAND ACKNOWLEDGMENT

The offices of *The Wayfarer Magazine* and Homebound Publications—the publishing company under which it falls—are situated in the small fishing village of Stonington, Connecticut on lands once occupied by the Pequot and the Mohegan people (known in present-day as the Mashantucket Pequot Tribal Nation and the Mohegan Nation respectively) whose lands were taken from them by force and duplicity. We honor this history and hold it within our minds and hearts as we midwife our creative endeavors from this space on the Connecticut shoreline.

The names of the land as quoted within this essay collection have gone by many names in the languages of both the native peoples for whom they were home and eventually the European settlers. But let us also remember that the land exists as a sentient being beyond labels, borders, and quantification.

WWW.THEWAYFARER.HOMEBOUNDPUBLICATIONS.COM

THE WAYFARER

RE-IMAGINING THE POSSIBLE ✦ CHARTING THE WAY FOR CHANGE

FOUNDER AND EDITOR-IN-CHIEF

L.M. Browning

MANAGING EDITOR

Heidi Barr

EDITORS

Theodore Richards

Eric D. Lehman

Amy Nawrocki

Iris Graville

EDITORS-AT-LARGE

Frank LaRue Owen Jr.

J.K. McDowell

Jason Kirkey

STAFF WRITERS

David K. Leff

Quinn Gathercole

READER

Marianne Browning

J.K. McDowell

CONTACT US

The Wayfarer Magazine

PO Box 1442, Pawcatuck CT 06379

thewayfarer@homeboundpublications.com

SUBSCRIBE

www.thewayfarer.homeboundpublications.com

or orders@homeboundpublications.com

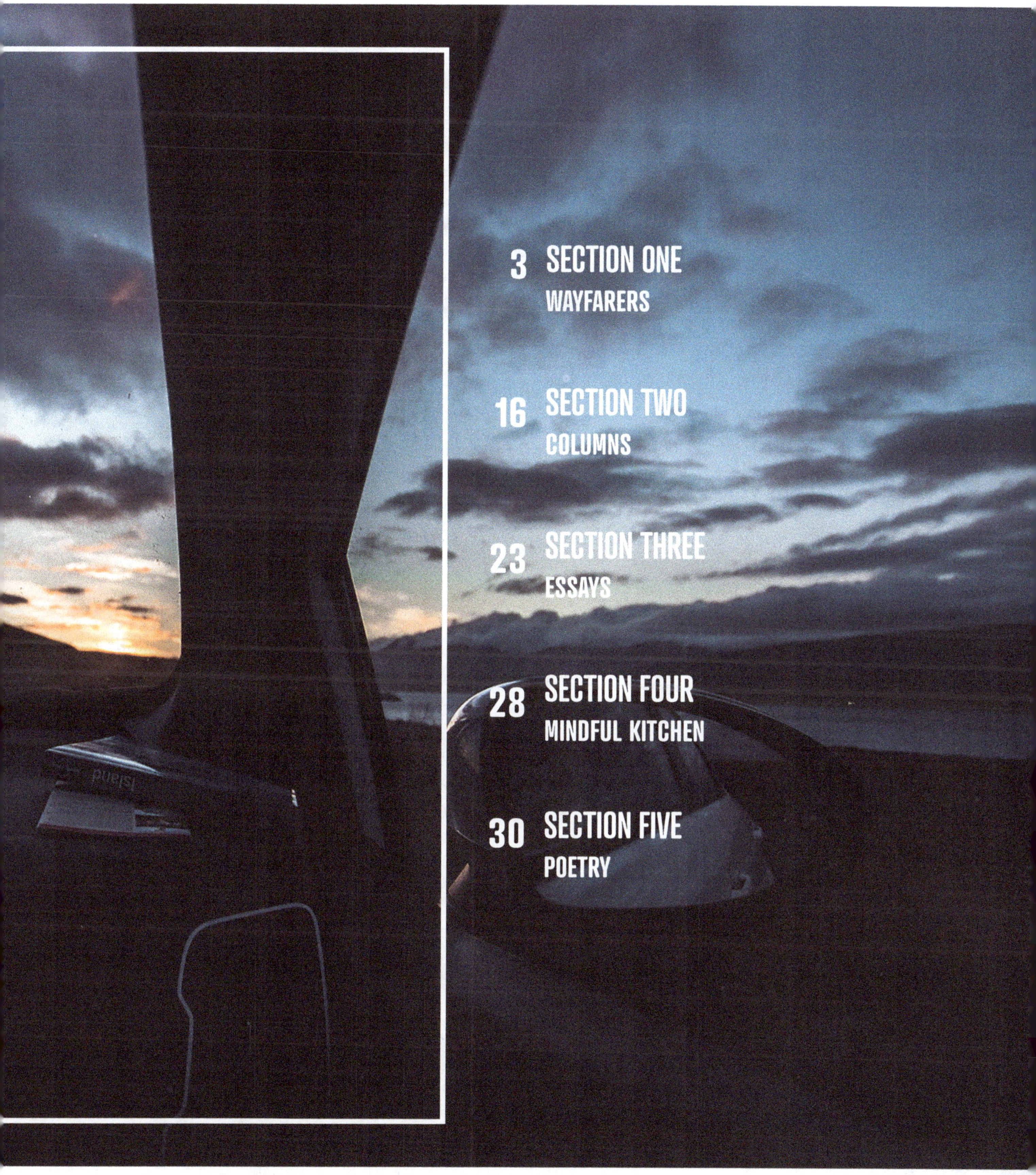

A *Posthumous Conversation with Wayfarer Rachel Carson*

by Editor Iris Graville

Nearly every issue of this journal includes interviews with *wayfarers*, described as those whose inner compass is ever-oriented to truth, wisdom, healing, and beauty in their own wandering. These stories of present-day writers, artists, activists, and spiritual leaders guide us in our own travels.

But what if we could time-travel to pose the burning questions of our times to wayfarers from the past? Kathleen Dean Moore did just that in her "posthumous interview" of Edward Abbey in *Great Tide Rising: Towards Clarity and Moral Courage in a Time of Planetary Change* (Counterpoint, 2016). Someone I'd want to converse with is Rachel Carson, an early writer about threats to the environment and author of *Silent Spring* (Houghton Mifflin, 1962).

One of Carson's early books, *The Sea Around Us* (Oxford University Press, 1951), serves as a biography of the sea, noted for both its science and its poetic prose. I found great inspiration from it for my essay collection, *Writer in a Life Vest: Essays from the Salish Sea* (2022, Homebound Publications). The Salish Sea desperately needs Carson right now, so I borrowed Moore's technique to devise my own questions to fit Carson's previously-published words for replies. I imagine our conversation going something like this.

*　　*　　*　　*

IRIS GRAVILLE: You're a well-respected thinker and writer about conservation, and you spent a lot of time studying the sea. What drew you to the ocean?

Bottom: Rachel Carson, 1940. U.S. Fish and Wildlife Service employee photo
Top: Iris Graville 2021

RACHEL CARSON: As long as I can remember, it [the sea] has fascinated me. Even as a child—long before I had ever seen it—I used to imagine what it would look like, and what the surf sounded like. Since I grew up in an inland community, where we hadn't even a migrating seagull, I had to wait a long time to have my curiosity satisfied. As a matter of fact, it wasn't until I had graduated from college and gone to Woods Hole [Marine Biological Laboratory] … that I saw the ocean. There, I began to get my first real understanding of the real sea world, that is, the world as it is known by shore-birds and fishes and beach crabs and all the other creatures that live in the sea or along its edge.[1] Fish, amphibian, and reptile, warm-blooded bird and mammal—each of us carries in our veins a salty stream in which the elements sodium, potassium, and calcium are combined in almost the same proportions as in seawater.[2]

IG: I live on the Salish Sea in Washington State. I feel both fortunate to live so close to the sea and distressed by the visible effects of climate change around me. But so many people don't live anywhere near an ocean. Why should they care?

RC: Even in the vast and mysterious reaches of the sea, we are brought back to the fundamental truth that nothing lives to itself.[3] Water must be thought of in terms of the chains of life it supports.[4]

IG: At the centennial of your birth, the United States House of Representatives passed a resolution in your honor. Here's one portion of the resolution:

Resolved, That the House of Representatives— recognizes that we could learn much from her today, especially as we increasingly feel the effects of climate change and consider measures to lessen and eventually, reverse the impact it has on our planet.

What do you think is the most important learning we could gain from you today?

RC: We cannot think of the living organism alone; nor can we think of the physical environment as a separate entity. The two exist together, each acting on the other to form an ecological complex or an ecosystem. With these surface waters, through a series of delicately adjusted, interlocking relationships, the life of all parts of the sea is linked. What happens to a diatom in the upper, sunlit strata of the sea may well determine what happens to a cod lying on a ledge of some rocky canyon a hundred fathoms below, or to a bed of multicolored, gorgeously plumed sea worms carpeting an underlying shoal, or to a prawn creeping over the soft oozes of the sea floor in the blackness of mile-deep water.[5]

IG: It seems the more we learn, the more complicated the natural world is, and the more unattainable renewal is. How did we get here, and how can we change?

RC: We behave, not like people guided by scientific knowledge, but more like the proverbial bad housekeeper who sweeps the dirt under the rug in the hope of getting it out of sight. We dump wastes of all kinds into our streams, with the object of having them carried away from our shores. We discharge the smoke and fumes of a million smokestacks and burning rubbish heaps into the atmosphere in the hope that the ocean of air is somehow vast enough to contain them. Now, even the sea has become a dumping ground, not only for assorted rubbish, but for the poisonous garbage of the atomic age. And this is done, I repeat, without recognition of the fact that introducing harmful substances into the environment is not a one-step process. It is changing the nature of the complex ecological system and is changing it in ways that we usually do not foresee until it is too late. This lack of foresight is one of the most serious complications, I think. It is not half so important to know as to feel. The more clearly we can focus our attention on the wonders and realities of the universe about us, the less taste we shall have for destruction.[6]

Iris Graville is the author of four nonfiction books: *Writer in a Life Vest, Hands at Work, BOUNTY,* and a memoir, *Hiking Naked.* She lives on Lopez Island, WA where she publishes SHARK REEF Literary Magazine, writes essays and blogs, and teaches. irisgraville.com.

IG: It can be difficult for people to believe that climate change is truly a crisis and that we humans are responsible for it. It's as if we're unwilling to look at the damage we continue to cause. How would you convince us to take this destruction seriously?

RC: In spite of the truly marvelous inventiveness of the human brain, we are beginning to wonder whether our power to change the face of nature should not have been tempered with wisdom for our own good, and with a greater sense of responsibility for the welfare of generations to come. Contrary to the beliefs that seem often to guide our actions, man does not live apart from the world; he lives in the midst of a complex, dynamic interplay of physical, chemical, and biological forces, and between himself and this environment there are continuing, never-ending interactions. One way to open your eyes is to ask yourself—What if I had never seen this before? What if I knew I would never see it again?[7]

IG: You received the National Book Award for *The Sea Around Us*, and it was described as poetic. Do you think of your writing as poetry?[9]

RC: If there is poetry in my book about the sea, it is not because I deliberately put it there, but because no one could write truthfully about the sea and leave out the poetry.[8]

IG: I'm deeply grateful for your writings about the ocean and environmental protection. Composing essays and poems is my response to the climate crisis, but I often question if that's of any use. What are your thoughts about the value of creative writing?

RC: The aim of science is to discover and illuminate truth. And that, I take it, is the aim of literature.[9] A good deal of poetry and stories have been focused on the sea, and quite a bit of science as well. But the best writing combines the two. The books that influence—that push movements forward—are the books that marry science and emotion.[10]

IG: Every day, news reports about repealed environmental policies, extinction of animals, wildfires, oil spills, and rising seas frighten and wear me (and many others) down. How do we keep our spirits up?

RC: Those who contemplate the beauty of the earth find reserves of strength that will last as long as life lasts. There is something infinitely healing in the repeated refrains of nature—the assurance that dawn comes after night and spring after winter.[11]

IG: Thank you, Ms. Carson. Your inner compass continues to be a crucial guide.

1- 2 Carson, Rachel. *The Sea Around Us*. Oxford: Oxford University Press, 1951.
3 - 4 Carson, Rachel. *Silent Spring*. New York: Houghton Mifflin, 1962.
5 Carson, Rachel. *The Sea Around Us*. Oxford: Oxford University Press, 1951.
6 Excerpt from acceptance speech for the John Burroughs Medal in 1952 for The Sea Around Us.
7 Carson, Rachel. The Sense of Wonder. New York: Harper Collins, 1956.
8 Carson, Rachel. The Sea Around Us. Oxford: Oxford University Press, 1951.
9 Lear, Linda, ed. Lost Woods: The Discovered Writing of Rachel Carson. Boston: Beacon Press, 1998.
10 Excerpt from acceptance speech for the National Book Award in 1952 for The Sea Around Us.
11 Carson, Rachel. Silent Spring. New York: Houghton Mifflin, 1962.

MAKING ART ALONE & TOGETHER

A CONVERSATION BETWEEN WAYFARER EDITORS, AMY NAWROCKI & ERIC D. LEHMAN

Eric Lehman: Let's start by talking about how we came to writing.

Amy Nawrocki: When I was younger, I had romantic ideas of what a writer was. I thought about trying to be a writer while I was in high school. I loved literature; I read Vonnegut; I read Virginia Woolf. What do you need to write? Well, *A Room of One's Own*. So, I had a very romantic idea and wanted to write to have that life—to be a "writer." And I wanted to write novels, to write fiction, because that is what I was reading.

Eric: I had a similar romantic ideal when I was in high school. I wanted to write poetry, so we've switched. Let me put it this way, I thought I had talent. I was told I had talent.

Amy: By whom?

Eric: Teachers, mostly. Classmates. At any rate, that all changed when I read *Tropic of Cancer* my freshman year of college. At that point, I didn't want to be a famous poet anymore; I wanted to reach people. I wanted to change things with my writing. Which is motivation, but it doesn't help you actually write. That changed again when I became a teacher: I wanted to teach people with my writing, which can be problematic, as well. For my travel writing, I want to communicate my experiences, and make other people consider their own experiences. I write philosophical essays and of course those are pedantic: I want to explain a topic like friendship or culture.

Amy: That's connected to your experience. For you, I think it's that idea about communicating information—getting people to think about their own ideas.

Eric: I have experiences that I have learned from, truths that I've come across in my life, and I want to get that across to others. But everyone knows you can't teach wisdom. So, what am I really doing?

Amy: Maybe "teach" is the wrong word. Communicate experience might be a better phrase. For me, communicating experience would be a reason to write. That's literature. To have experience, to participate in others' experience, is one of the reasons we read. It's a sustained connection. Would you say that's your overall reason? To get people to realize where they are, who they are, and to be more conscious?

Eric: To increase awareness. Of course, all written language does that; it increases our awareness in a different way, adds a dimension to the lived world. But if I'm honest, I also have a more selfish reason for doing it, to become a master writer, so to speak. To develop my sense of self.

Amy: What role does creative work play in developing a sense of self?

Eric: I think it's absolutely vital. It changes memory; it focuses things; it forces you to pay attention to things in a different way.

Amy: You're not just a participant; you're a recorder; you're recording things for use later. You're paying attention to things. Because I create things, I want to be more aware of things. I want to share.

Eric: Exactly. So that's changing the whole aspect of you. And when you put pen to paper it forces you to focus everything into that language.

"FOR ME, COMMUNICATING EXPERIENCE WOULD BE A REASON TO WRITE. THAT'S LITERATURE. TO HAVE EXPERIENCE, TO PARTICIPATE IN OTHERS' EXPERIENCE, IS ONE OF THE REASONS WE READ. IT'S A SUSTAINED CONNECTION. WOULD YOU SAY THAT'S YOUR OVERALL REASON? TO GET PEOPLE TO REALIZE WHERE THEY ARE, WHO THEY ARE, AND TO BE MORE CONSCIOUS?" —AMY NAWROCKI

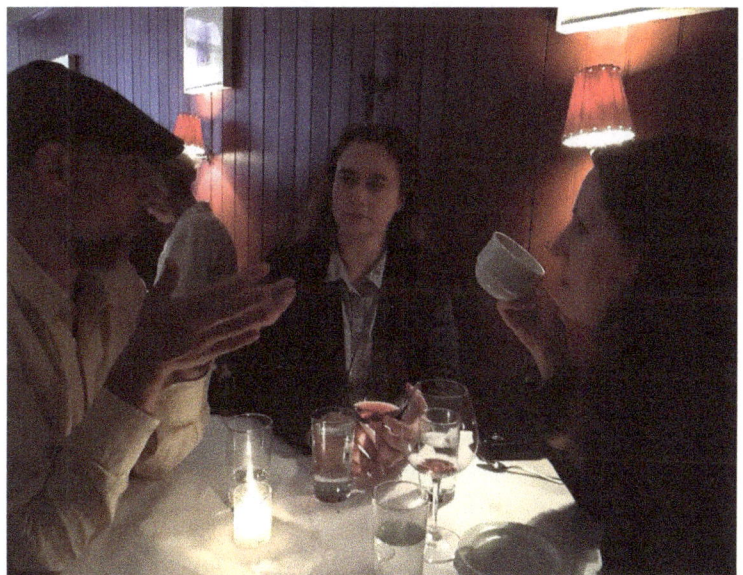

Amy: I would agree with that, though I would argue that it's not the only way to develop a sense of self. I think any discipline can do that. But art it certainly one of them. To be clear, though, what does "sense of self" mean for you?

Eric: A sense of individuality. Uniqueness.

Amy: A sense that you're different from everyone: you're different from your siblings, your friends; you're different from your parents.

Eric: Yes. It gives you a sense that you are doing something worthwhile, too. Writing sometimes gives me a hope that what I am doing might contribute to humanity.

Amy: I've always thought of a sense of self somewhat differently. It's very internal for me—the idea of who am I. It's not something that I can really pinpoint—how that is or what it is. I'm sure I thought about how I can contribute to the world, but I've never thought of self in that way. It's an understanding of who you are.

Eric: That's interesting, almost backwards to what I said: you build a sense of self, and then your sense of self builds your creativity, your creative work. Either way, that forward motion is another reason I am a writer. It is satisfying to work on a skill to become an expert, to become someone who's achieved the highest level possible. Someone who pushes the boundaries of language, the conventions of structure.

Amy: As we've passed through modernism, or post modernism, whatever you want to call it, the boundaries have already been pushed. How far do you push them? There are people who are no longer writing in verse or meter; they're pushing it so far that it's not even recognizable as poetry anymore. Language itself is evolving. That's great, but where do you think you fit in?

Eric: I'd rather push the boundaries of certain genres. For example, what I've done with history books, weaving history into narrative, or vice versa, impressed a few editors over the years. One said that out of the hundreds and hundreds of books that she'd gone through, my work was different. That's a small way of pushing the boundary. When I write fantasy and science fiction novels, I try to push the boundaries structurally while maintaining a narrative voice. So, maybe I am developing my own cross-genre writing style that will end up being associated with me.

Amy: Now that you've developed that as a style, do you feel that you need to push the boundaries beyond that to something different or new?

Eric: I don't know.

Amy: When I get a little bit bored with my own style—for example, longer lines with unbroken stanzas, I change it up, make the lines shorter, try a three-line stanza, write in the voice of a child rather than a woman. It's not necessarily wanting to push a boundary, it's just I'm a little tired with what I've been doing lately. If you set out to "push boundaries" you're probably going to fail. You shouldn't think of things in a grandiose way. You can't think that "I'm going to develop a new style," or "I'm going to come up with a new way to write paragraphs." You have to say, "I'd like to try this a different way today. And look, that worked or that didn't." Perhaps that idea of pushing boundaries simply means finding something new and exploring it.

Eric: Let's get a little more specific. Do you have a clear idea of what you are writing from the outset?

Amy: I have had experiences where the end result may have changed radically from where I started, but I usually start by sitting down and saying, "Okay, I think I know what I want to say in this poem, and I think I know, at least partly, how to say it." It starts with some kind of idea. But that idea can be fairly amorphous and unshaped. Only a couple of times has the idea that I started with stayed true to the idea that I ended with. When I wrote a poem about the shipwreck we found on Cape Cod, I had an idea in my mind, and it came from Adrienne Rich's poem "Diving into the Wreck." We had seen this ancient wreck, and it was such a compelling experience. Her poem was a parallel starting place, and then I worked to get to where the poem is something new, and for me satisfying. Present experience and past reading came together.

Eric: Remember how the timber frame didn't use nails? That was an old ship.

Amy: Yes, and when the details are so observably interesting, it's a decent enough starting point.

Eric: Anyway, for me, a similar piece is my novella *Shadows of Paris*, most of which I wrote when we were actually in Paris. Now, like you, I had an idea even before we went to Paris of the type of story I wanted to write. It's a structural trope: a person goes to a place and is healed at that place. I probably got the idea from a book called *A Month in the Country*.

Amy: That too points to the influence of other writers.

Eric: Yes, let's come back to that. So, I had that idea and I then went to Paris with you and that first full day we walked down the hill and walked into Notre Dame and sat in the transept. Then I started to write, and every day on that trip I wrote. I was being inspired, and that's important. But the ideas had a structure to work into. When we got home, I did hard work: I revised and edited it. I think also I was in a position that I could write that; I had written five terrible books already and had studied literature my whole life. Let's say I was writing a scene where William meets Lucy in the bookstore. What do I have to know to write that scene? I have to know many places like that and be able to describe it. I have to know how to write atmosphere, how to be able to build character so that we immediately know Lucy, not just through what she looks like, but through her actions. I didn't have to go to Paris to write that scene, but I did have to read a hundred books. I had to practice that type of character building. It's not like I was thinking about those things when I wrote that, necessarily. Those things were already a part of me.

Amy: We had input that was different from everyday life. I mean it was Paris, for Keats' sake.

Eric: You wrote some of your best poems there.

Amy: We were in a magical place. We were following in the footsteps of all these great artists and writers, you know going to places that they had been, sitting in cafés where Hemingway and others had written. It

was inspiring and you feel part of a writing community. And you did something similar with the places in *9 Lupine Road: A Supernatural Tale on the Tracks of Kerouac*. You took places like the crooked cabin and Oxnard from our own history, and the places and people from the Beat generation, and mixed them together.

Eric: Would you say that applies to you, too? What about your poem "Ravens of West Rock" in *Mouthbrooders*?

Amy: For sure. It's a poem about entering into a landscape that is part reality and part literary interchange. You can't witness a raven without hearing echoes of Edgar Allen Poe. But it's more than that. If you just acknowledge that you're examining your life, an authentic life, then that authenticity comes from acknowledgement of the decision. You acknowledge that and then say, "now I'm going to work to make this the best thing I could possibly do during this moment in my life."

Eric: That's a great way of thinking about it. Let's come back to the influence of other writers. Specifically, the influence we have had on each other. We've helped each other edit and revise and have actually written four books together, books that have both our names on them. Often, the narrative we hear is that two writers cannot be married, cannot work together, because of fame and jealousy. Hemingway and Gellhorn, Percy and Mary Shelley, et cetera. When early on in our relationship I realized you were a better poet than I was, for example, I expected some disaster of that sort to follow. But that hasn't been our experience at all. Likewise, I saw many artists who had failed relationships because their spouse or lover was outside their art, meaning they couldn't share in that kind of creation. So, I always thought that would happen with me. Instead, our relationship has helped me to produce more and better work.

Amy: The question came up earlier in this conversation: why do I write? I write for you. That's just as valid a reason as any other.

Eric: Of course, you write to impress somebody you love.

Amy: That's why so many authors tried to write. Dante wrote for Beatrice, Petrarch for Laura... That idea of having outside encouragement and inspiration. To have inside encouragement is one thing; to have someone outside encouraging you is another thing. It's motivating to have someone cheering you on, to say "keep going." Also, I write so that you will give me feedback and I will get better. I write to share to load when there's a collaborative project.

Eric: We've gone to a coffee shop and created side by side, we've both been writing, creating. Does that add, does that subtract to the artistic process, or is that extraneous? I wrote most of *Shadows of Paris* with you next to me, in the room, and I felt your presence was additive for that, it helped me create.

Amy: It's just another kind of audience. We lucked out having each other for both inspiration and encouragement. But all writing is collaborative.

Eric: Right. For a playwright or anyone who works in a collaborative medium the idea of a solitary artist is laughable. And of course, we all have influences, people who give input, help us edit, and inspire to one degree or another. But I'm not just talking about input. I'm talking about output, the action of it. Action itself is not a solitary act. Action defies solitariness. By creating you are defying solitariness.

Amy: Yeah, but in a metaphorical world. And I agree with you. I totally agree with you. I think you're right that when you create something you're thinking of an audience You're thinking of someone who will read this, someone will be moved by this, someone will have a thought from this. And of course, that is interactive, not solitary.

Eric: Right.

Amy: I think there's another element of it, where a faulty relationship comes in, or where artists go it alone, for whatever reasons. They don't find someone equally as interested in what they're doing as they are, and so they're isolated. Or just the act of creation is isolated because they're doing it by themselves. You're right in one way; you're not alone, because the act of producing is interactive, because

you're producing something someone will read. It's your imaginary audience in the room with you. But you are alone, you are solitary. It can be lonely.

Think about before you knew me. We both were solitary after grad school. Finding someone to write with is part of your evolution, of exploding the myth of the lonely artist you held onto. That's why people gravitate towards writing groups, or MFA programs, or conferences. That's why lawyers or doctors congregate together, because they have those things in common. But there's also a loneliness in the idea that whatever we produce as writers might never be read. Or that it won't be accepted, or appreciated, or lead to anything. We struggle with that because we're trying to get things published and keep pushing ourselves as writers. No one is seeing that struggle, and it's lonely. We get the sense were in this together, but nobody knows this work is out there.

Eric: I like the way you've separated this. You've pointed out that whether or not you are alone in your real life, you're not necessarily solitary: it's how you feel about it.

Amy: It's perception.

Eric: It's perception, right, and the reason for the perception is lack of understanding or acceptance, whatever terminology you want to use.

Amy: Maybe pushing the boundaries means reestablishing our connection to ourselves as writers, to our sense of self and how creativity is always collaborative, never solitary.

Eric: And that's the primary thing to avoid, right, because that's what causes a feeling of solitariness, and worse loneliness. You write because you are reaching out, because you know other people are there.

Amy: When you realize that you're not, in fact, alone or by yourself.

Eric: Right.

Amy: And that's the heart of how you live a happy life.

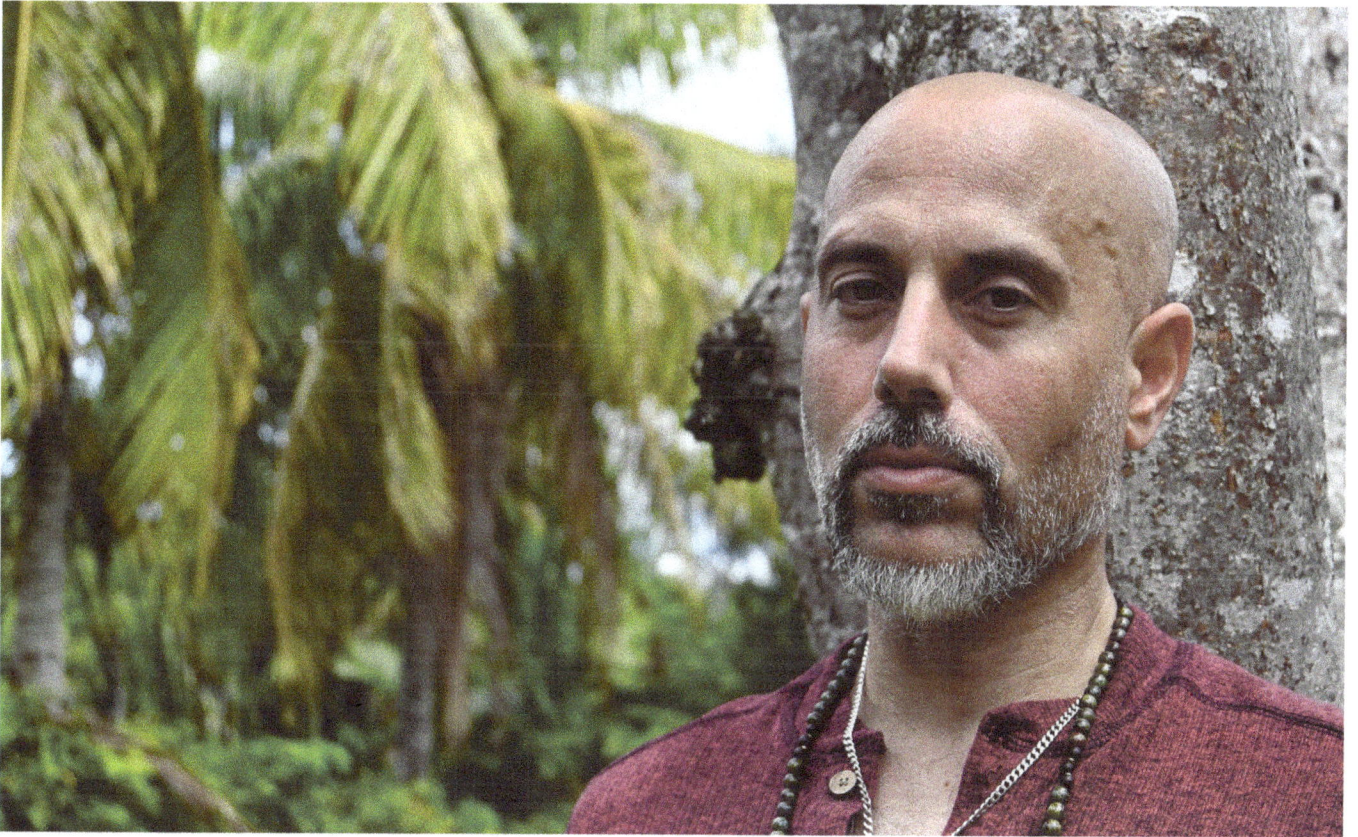

REIMAGINING

INTERVIEW WITH AUTHOR, PHILOSOPHER, AND EDUCATOR THEODORE RICHARDS
BY EDITOR, ERIC D. LEHMAN

Eric Lehman: We're talking about your writing life and real life and how these things intersect. How do you see your role as a writer in the world?

Theodore Richards: I believe strongly in the power of sharing stories. A lot of my work has been around exploring—on a philosophical and educational level—ways we can reimagine narratives and stories about our place in the world. That's what philosophy does, it engages people in different ways of seeing the world, asking different kinds of questions, and that's what education is, exploring different questions and different ways of seeing the world. I also see this moment as a really significant moment in human history when we need to think of new kinds of narratives.

EL: Your day job is as an educator. Do you see yourself as someone who educates through writing?

TR: The work I do now is teaching in higher education, philosophy mostly, but I've spent much of my life developing different ways of thinking about education for younger people. In the nonprofit that I started, The Chicago Wisdom Project, we work through holistic models with young people and try to create a space for them to reimagine a sense of who they are and their place in the world. What we do is allow them to think differently about who they are and give them the courage and the power to reimagine their own experience. It also empowers them to be teachers of others and create a learning space where everyone is teaching one another.

Some of my writing has been explicitly about that. As a philosopher the work I have done has been exploring cosmologies and worldviews from the past as a way to understand the worldview we hold today in the modern industrial world, and as a way to rethink that view.

EL: And you think that is the role of both education and literature?

TR: We often talk about what makes a good school or what makes a good teacher, but seldom do we ask the question: 'what is the whole point of this?' The argument I would make is that the bigger purpose of education is to give a person a sense of who they are. That is something that doesn't only happen in a school, but I think that what a school does is serve as a metaphor for a world that we want to create. If we create a space in which people are cared for, a place where people are seen and heard, where people's stories are honored, then that is the kind of world we are going to get. If we create a space in which people are just trying to get the highest grades, that will lead to another kind of world.

EL: Tell me specifically about your work with the Wisdom Project.

TR: In my thirties, I was in California studying and one of my teachers was the author, theologian, and activist Matthew Fox. He hired my wife and me to apply the holistic model he used for his graduate students to teenagers in Oakland. This was in the early days of No Child Left behind and there was a huge push to reduce all education in our schools to a discreet and narrow range of quantifiable outcomes. And we wanted to do the opposite.

Then in 2009 I returned to Chicago finishing up my PhD. I was very much an outsider in academia, I wasn't published yet, I didn't find any job openings for philosopher-poet on Craig's List or wherever you might look. So, I created my own job. I had lots of experience working with young people in Chicago and I knew I could get a similar program to Fox's off the ground. It's the sort of education that the most privileged children get, in which they are encouraged to explore, to be inquisitive, to examine their place in the world, and to ask questions. We wanted to give that to these less privileged students on the south side of Chicago.

Today, we have grown and seeded projects in other cities. We recently merged with the Baltimore Wisdom Project, into Wisdom Projects, Inc. We continue to have youth programs, but we also have a different focus, to develop curriculum and approaches to learning that engage the whole person.

EL: In your work itself you draw a lot of inspiration from travel. How do you see travel as part of education and philosophy?

What I gained from travel was that I saw firsthand different ways of seeing the world and recognized that the way I'd been taught wasn't the only possibility. Doing this in the days before GPS and cellphones and any kind of connectivity, forced me to confront some of the more difficult elements of our world, some of the suffering and despair. And when you are far away you are also forced to confront things in yourself.

For example, once when I was working as an aid worker in rural Zimbabwe, I was tasked by the NGO I worked for to teach classes to women living in rural villages. They gave us very specific times, a class at 9 and a class at 1, and they told us to start on time. But this was a place without electricity and clocks, so no one had any conception of this

European notion of time. People would show up when they were able to show up. It wasn't that people were less capable of understanding, they just had a completely different view of the world. Time had to do with things they had to accomplish, of the natural cycles around them, so people showed up to class when they'd fed their children or tended their crops or fetched water from the river. This thing we think is an absolute reality, this notion of time that we have on our phones, is a construct in our culture like any other construct. So that was a genuine difference in worldview that I experienced directly and it was really enlightening.

EL: Some people might see your work as a writer and an educator as political. Do you see yourself or your work in that way?

TR: In a secondary way. I certainly don't see it as apolitical and I'm not afraid of that label. There are certainly political elements to it. For me, good philosophy cannot be so abstract and distant from the world that it does not engage in real world questions and problems and in that way it must intersect with the political. I would suggest that the same could be said about education. It needs to engage with real world matters that affect us.

One of the things that is getting lost in our public education system—not across the board but in many cases as we move towards teaching specific skill sets—is that we are losing touch with this notion that public schools ought to be a place where people learn how to participate in a democracy. If you're going to have a public education system, it seems to me that teaching people to engage in a democracy would be fundamental to that.

EL: I can see a lot of your work as spiritual as well as philosophical. Do you see any difference between those two things?

TR: My background is in religion and religious studies as a philosopher, so for me philosophy helps to have a deeper understanding of spiritual practices and principles. The difference might be that the spiritual part is where we do the actual inner work and the philosophical part would be understanding. But I see those as two sides of the same coin.

EL: Great distinction.

TR: While there is a distinction, they are best in concert. Too often we have weak philosophical understanding of spiritual practices or religious dogma. It's useful to have a deeper understanding of those ideas to engage more honestly in spiritual practice. On the other side, understanding something intellectually while useful and meaningful can be deepened and enhanced by also engaging in some of that personal inner work. Many of my philosophical ideas have come through practice and been in in dialogue with practice.

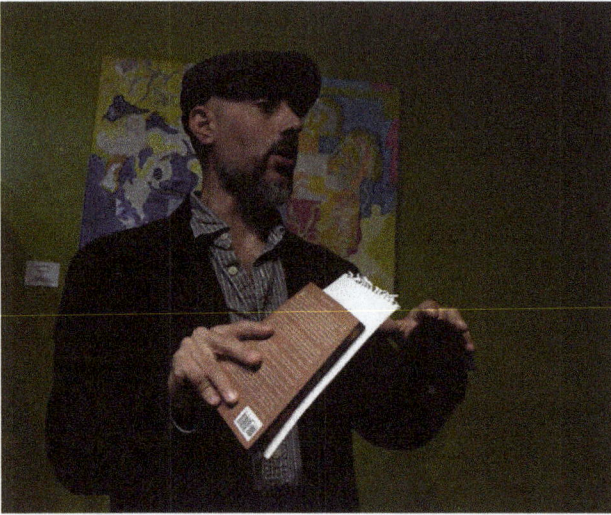

EL: My favorite book of yours is *A Letter to My Daughters*. One of the things that makes it so strong is your speaking to your daughters. How does being a father impact your writing?

TR: Everything in my life has been informed by having children. It's helped me to be able to see the world through a different lens. Watching my children engage in the world through play—how all children engage the world—for me is the model for any kind of innovative art or ideas or new ways of being in the world. Even the dialogue we're having now is play. Picking up a backpack is play. And sitting down and writing a book is play. Playfulness is a pathway to create new worlds, which children do every day, and then they break it all down and start again each morning.

Earlier, I mentioned that there's some value to seeing the suffering in the world—I don't know if that's helpful if we can't also see the joy. Fatherhood has helped me to see the joy.

EL: You write in a number of different genres—fiction, nonfiction, philosophy—and at the same time you also write about different subjects. How are these connected?

TR: My work as an educator and as a writer and as a philosopher is thinking through the different ways of understanding our world, and as a writer of fiction or poetry, storytelling, narrative driven work, we can get at the heart of seeing the world through another person's eyes. So many things in our world would be better if we could see the world through others' eyes. Right now it seems like we're all struggling with what lens to look through, and I think that's the common thread through the work. How can we reimagine the world we are seeing right now? I suggest that if we look at any of the larger crises we're facing—climate change for example—it is not a lack of technical knowhow or scientific information that makes it difficult. Our shared story and what our purpose is in the world kind of gets in the way of living more sustainably.

EL: You keep using the phrase "reimagining," and you have a magazine and podcast of that title. Tell me about how that grew out of what you do.

TR: *Reimagining* is an online magazine and podcast for the Wisdom Projects, Inc. We've brought in some really interesting guests and asked them how they are seeking to reimagine the world through their work. We've brought in folks who are doing work in various areas, from education to therapy, and created a space for our students, poets, and thinkers of all different backgrounds to do work that challenges our core values and narratives.

EL: You've mentioned Matthew Fox as a mentor. What other mentors or influences do you have?

TR: As a philosophy graduate student, I worked with both Matthew Fox and Brian Swimme. My ideas about cosmology come from Brian, who collaborated a lot with cultural historian Thomas Berry. I also had a martial arts teacher who I studied Bagua with for many years and I was influenced by a woman named Sue Duncan, who ran an afterschool program here in Chicago. As far as writers, I love Dante and James Baldwin is just about the best essayist you could find. I've been lucky to have mentors; many people don't have any. Mentors are important.

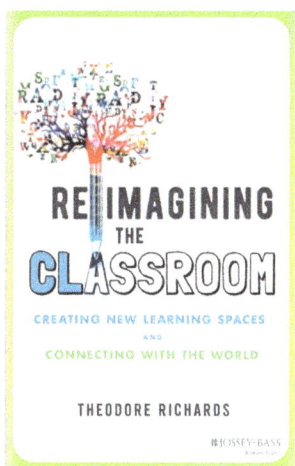

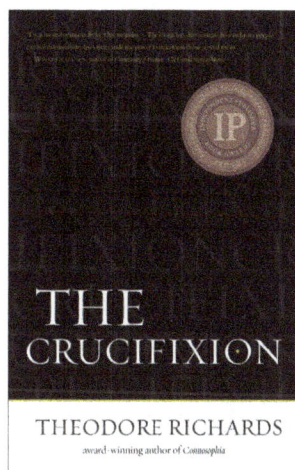

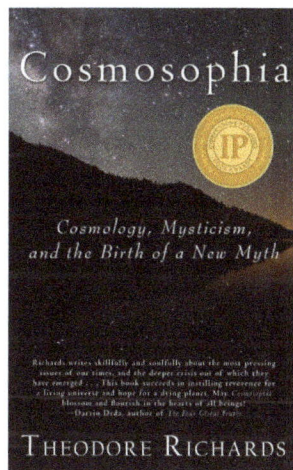

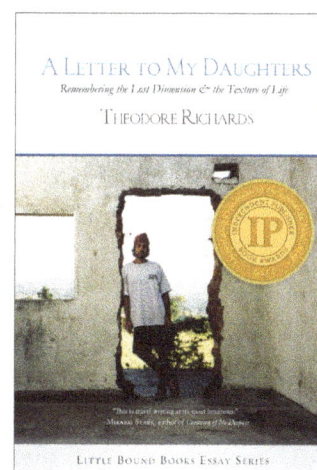

You need someone who's not your parents who can be a mentor. We substitute it with coaches or teachers but so often these people are only with you for a year.

I grew up playing sports and often the coach-player relationship is toxic. Sometimes people have coaches who are mentors who stay with them but not often. With my kids, it is so important for them to have 'aunties' who are not us. Full grown adults. My 13-year-old is at the stage of life where she does not want to listen to what we are telling her. It's normal. What she does need though is another adult she can talk to or listen to.

EL: It's missing in American culture.

TR: Yes, all the mentors I named were young adulthood and beyond. I could have used more as a teenager. We're also definitely saturated with bad examples. I retained certain things I had been shown that were unhealthy. Things to avoid. But what you need the positive examples, too.

EL: You have *Reimagining* and the Homebound family. How important is being part of a community of writers to you?

TR: More and more I come to see the importance of community to all we do in life. As a writer, because it is fundamentally solitary activity, it is good to

have other people you can talk to. All those relationships you have, those come into your work as a writer, all the books that you read, all the people that influence you, if someone ever asks you how you improve your writing, generally, you say live a rich life and read good books. Part of a rich life is having other writers in your life. On a fundamental level I increasingly recognize that having other people to share what we're going through is so important, it's the only way we can take care of each other.

The act of writing is the final act as a writer. The rest of the work is what happens in the remainder of your life.

EL: How do you want your work as a writer or human being to resonate a hundred years from now?

TR: Two things. First, I would like for people to gain a sense of a new story and a process to get to that new story. And the second thing is that I would like people to recognize my journey moving from a person who was taught at a young age that we are fundamentally alone to being a person who lives and moves in the world in relationship to others. And how that journey is not easy, because it challenges some of the most basic assumptions that we have about our place in the world.

CONNECTING THE DOTS

THE ENVIRONMENTAL COLUMN BY GAIL COLLINS-RANADIVE

Standing at my dining room window watching the last of the New Year's Eve fireworks explode over the Las Vegas Strip, I turned to my partner, kissed him a Happy 2022, and asked if we should start banging our heads against the wall right then and there. Or should we wait until the light of day, as another year began ticking towards the irreversible deadline to deal with climate change.

The year that the climate changed dramatically had just ended with ferocious winds blowing burning embers through two drought-dry Colorado towns, blow-torching a thousand homes just hours ahead of the area's first snow storm, after a summer of no rain or rainbows along the Front Range.

Beginning with the Texas February freeze and continuing through the intense summer heat in the Pacific Northwest, Hurricane Ida in the Gulf, massive California wildfires, and the mid-December tornado outbreak across the center of the country, all these (and more) measurable climate-change fingerprints cost the 2021 economy billions of dollars in climate-related disasters.

Clearly climate change is not coming: it is here.

On last summer's day that the United Nation's Intergovernmental Panel on Climate Change declared "Code Red for Humanity," I took my angst out to a nearby greenspace. Because the natural world has been my 'go to' place for clarity and comfort since childhood, I needed to see the Indian Paintbrush that grew on a tiny patch of wildness beside the well-worn dirt path. But as I searched for the familiar scarlet spears, the only red I saw was the wildfire caused smoky red eye of the rising sun on my left, while on my right red tail lights lit up on the back of the idling construction vehicle. Its driver was waiting for the rest of the paving crew to arrive, and meanwhile spewing toxins and pollutants into the air being breathed-in by us runners, walkers, and cyclists.

Standing between them, I could spread my arms and connect the dots between the cause and effect of the existential crisis currently threatening humankind.

We have known for decades what was coming if we don't stop burning fossil fuels. But now the IPCC has concluded that "the consequences are coming faster than predicted, and the earth is now almost certain to warm 1.5 degrees Celsius (2.7 degrees Fahrenheit) within the next two decades, and this warming will trigger even more extreme weather events than we have already been experiencing..." If we don't act immediately, the report, continues, "we could see another 4 degrees of warming compared with the preindustrial era."

As climate activists who have been trying to raise the alarm around what's happening and urge action, we've modelled what can be done on a personal level by reducing our carbon footprint. To get off coal generated electricity we put solar panels on our rooftops. To get off natural gas for home heating and cooling we installed geothermal and air sourced heat pumps. To get off oil for transportation we drive a plug-in electric car.

Our public actions have included writing books and essays, giving sermons and workshops, divesting, demonstrating, protesting, changing out a lawn for native, carbon capturing plants. Yet over the last decade, we've seen no downward turn in the amount of heat-trapping greenhouse gasses being emitted and trapped in the atmosphere.

Another international climate summit had come and gone, ending in the *'blah, blah, blah'* of empty promises, as youth activist Greta Thunberg put it.

And although 7 million more Americans voted for the presidential candidate who promised climate action than for the climate denying incumbent, whose policies had pushed the country backwards for four years, the new administration's climate legislation was being blocked by a Congressional majority beholden to fossil fuel interests.

As 2021 ended, we two were frankly at the end of our hope;

I had no idea how or if I could continue to keep on keeping on....banging my head against the wall of indifference and inaction had gotten old...yet what else was there to do in 2022? Might as well get started sooner rather than later....

Instead, we decided to wait until after we watched the much talked about film, Don't Look Up. We'd have to sign up for Netflix first, and Milt would have to stream it from his computer to my ancient television set, but I offered to cash-in my pandemic-Christmas 'I owe you' and spring for the film.

Nearly everything on my current Facebook feed was about the movie's connecting the dots between the corruption and complicity of corporate, media, and political 'responses' to an incoming comet. In short, it seemed to answer Neil deGrasse Tyson's question to us during his remake of Carl Sagans' Cosmos:

"The dinosaurs never saw that asteroid coming. What's our excuse?"

How could we not watch it?!

What an amazing way to begin 2022! No wonder climate scientists had been tweeting that they finally felt heard! We laughed and cried and high-fived each other throughout the entire film to the 'end,' then on through the credits and beyond, to a final scene of a satisfying, if ludicrous, vindication.

Afterwards, I took a 'processing' walk through the neighborhood, looking for the other-than-humans living among us: the owls that call in the dawn then sleep in a towering pine tree, the doves that keep watch from our rooftops, the ever-present rabbits that make us feel less alone, the quail family that stitches the neighborhood together, and the elusive coyote that keeps it all in balance.

Among the most heart-wrenching scenes in the film were brief views of the rest of planetary life. Now unwittingly at the mercy of a handful of humans in the global north who are driven by political power and corporate greed, the inhabitants of the global south, innocent children, indigenous peoples, and non-human species alike have been damned. Anyone who survives the increasingly severe droughts, fires,

Gail Collins-Ranadive, MA, MFA, MDIV, is the author of 9 published books, 5 through Homebound that include *Chewing Sand, Nature's Calling, A Fistful of Stars, Dinosaur Dreaming, Inner Canyon, Where Deep Time Meets Sacred Space* and the forthcoming: *Light Year; A Seasonal Guide for Eco-Spiritual Growth.* She also sponsors Homebound's Prism Prize for Climate Literature.

floods, tornadoes, hurricanes, tsunamis, sinking cities, will be confronted with famine, pandemics, and shrinking living space. Disrupted ecosystems will eventually push us over the cliff edge of extinction. Meanwhile, the three richest white men in the world are already testing their get-away rockets: after trashing this planet they'd simply leave it to live on another.

Yet, unlike the film's six-month timeline to comet-caused-annihilation, the coming climate apocalypse has a projected deadline of just under a decade.

We still have time to act.

I am old enough to remember ducking under desks in grade school during the cold war, hiding from the threat of a nuclear bomb, then questioning the government's assurance that we could sweep radioactive ash out of our homes with a broom. Many of us 'desk duckers' eventually organized the anti-nuclear movement, and slowed down the march towards Mutually Assured Destruction.

Could this holiday film carrying us into 2022 be a game-changer?

Could enough people be moved to connect the dots between comet and climate, and adamently demand and take action before it's too late?

Approaching my front door, I saw a small feather beside the welcome mat. Picking it up as a positive omen, I walked into the house, calling out to my partner: "Okay, I'm game. Sign me up for another year!"

"WHAT HAPPENED TO ICARUS?"

THE CONTEMPLATIVE COLUMN BY THEODORE RICHARDS

I want to know what happened to Icarus
after his wings melted away,
When he fell into the fathomless sea.
This is where the story begins.

The Greeks, as is their tendency, tell a good tale, of the boy, Icarus, who, in a quintessential act of hubris, flies too close to the sun, but they tell only part of the story. Icarus falls. We know this much. We know that his wings melted because he wouldn't listen to the wisdom of an elder, because he was too enraptured by the joy of his flight. Because he thought he could be a like a god. And most of us, eventually, come to know what this is like. We all, at some point, fly too close to the sun. We all fall. And we assume that Icarus dies. Indeed, his father, Daedalus, mourns him. This is treated as the end of the story. But perhaps we've missed something here. Perhaps, Daedalus mourns something in ourselves that dies when we fly too close to the sun, when we fall. We are forced—and we are all forced, eventually—to enter into the depths. The sea is ourselves. And, perhaps, Icarus's story truly begins when he goes below the surface.

I am thinking of all this, perhaps, because the recent years of my own life have been something like this fall. I am like Dante, in those famous first lines of the *Commedia*, embarking on "*il mezzo del cammin di nostra vita*"—the middle of the journey of our life. I have entered, as Dante had, the "*selva oscura*"—the dark wood. Dante writes these lines in exile, a forty-year-old man without a home. In his great work, he writes these lines as he enters the *inferno*. Dante understood that the most important work happens after we fall. It happens when we enter the depths—call it the sea or the *inferno*—and confront our deepest fears and longings, pain and joy.

Our ancient ancestors knew this when they crawled deep into caves and created masterpieces on the walls. They could have painted on the side of a cliff, or a tree, but they chose to crawl deep inside of the earth. Their pictures were at once cosmic and psychic, maps of soul and world, of womb and sky. I suspect that they intuited the significance of interiority, of going into the depths to find the answers to life's biggest questions.

Recent years of my life have involved challenges both personal and professional, of family and of community. I've lived through a pandemic, through streets on fire in protest and despair. Personally, I've had to confront my own greatest fears. For some of us, it takes until we reach middle age, until our wings have melted and we fall, in order to confront those demons. But however we get there, this is the real work of life. It's not the sort of stuff that shows up on a resume, or if you google yourself. But it's the most important work we'll ever do.

Much has been said, lately, about the crisis of mental health that corresponds to the physical health crisis (the pandemic, among other things) and the planetary health crisis (climate change). We are not only suffering from having sick bodies on a sick planet. Entangled in all this is the sickness of our inner lives. We are a depressed and lonely species. But we are beginning to see, finally, that we have to begin to be vulnerable with each other in order to see one another and in order to heal and grow.

This is important for us as individuals. We work through our trauma and heal only when we have the courage to travel to those depths. And this is especially important for boys and men. I can recall, at some point in my life, believing that to be a man meant that I wouldn't cry any more. It's really the opposite, of course. What we need, so desperately, are men and boys who know how to feel, how to love and to be loved. How to cry. As a parent and as an educator, I have come to believe that this is perhaps the most important thing we can teach our children.

And ours is also an age of collective trauma. Confronted with myriad challenges and despair, from climate change to the pandemic, we are at a moment of apocalypse and transformation. The old stories are dying; new ones are waiting to be born. And this requires nothing short of a shared shamanic journey, a death—like Icarus in the sea—and rebirth. But our new stories can only be birthed if we learn how to enter into the depths together, if we, like Daedalus, can learn to mourn authentically for what we've lost.

We have to learn to share our stories, our pain, our tears with one another because this is the only way we can take care of each other.

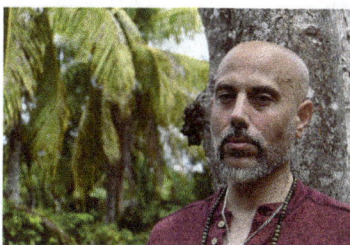

Theodore Richards (www.theodorerichards.com) is the founder of The Chicago Wisdom Project (www.chicagowisdomproject.org) and the author of seven books and numerous literary awards, including three Independent Book Awards and two Nautilus Book Awards. His most recent book is *A Letter to My Daughters: Remembering the Lost Dimension & the Texture of Life*, winner of the Independent Publisher Awards Gold Medal in memoir. He lives on the south side of Chicago with his wife and three daughters.

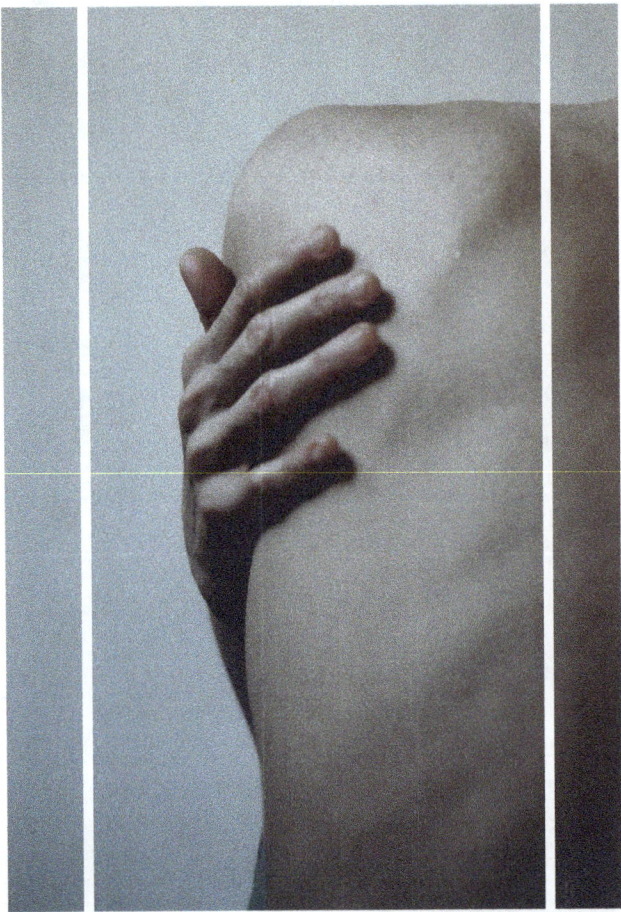

"YOU EITHER WALK
INSIDE YOUR STORY
AND OWN IT OR YOU
STAND OUTSIDE YOUR
STORY AND HUSTLE
FOR YOUR WORTHINESS."
—BRENE BROWN

TO FIND THE AUTHENTIC SELF
BY QUINN GATHERCOLE

I sit in my camping chair, staring excessively hard at the firewood as it burns in the pit. I can feel the beginnings of an idea slowly forming in the back of my mind. I'm listening to a pod cast conversation between Brene Brown and Laverne Cox. They are discussing the lack of positive representation of trans people in Hollywood. I hadn't ever really given it a lot of thought, but started to pay attention when I watched the documentary Laverne Cox produced back in January 2020. In the past, trans people were portrayed as the butt of a joke such as someone cross dressing to get a laugh, as the victim of a homicide by an outraged would-be lover, or by someone who was considered to have a mental illness. Not great representation at all, so it is refreshing that Hollywood is starting to make a change in how trans people are starting to be portrayed for the better.

Maybe I was a little late to the podcast since I was listening to it in the Fall of 2021, but I was scrolling through my list of podcasts while on a solo camping trip and was compelled to listen to it. So, I popped in my earbuds, sipped on my tea, and settled in. I chuckled when they brought up Buffalo Bill from *Silence of the Lambs*. Why would I chuckle at such a thing you might ask? Because it was the only way I was able to best describe to a friend what "non-binary" was when I was coming out. Imagine! How depraved is it that all I had to refer to was a serial killer from a psychological horror film who stalked, kidnapped, starved, and murdered women to make a body suit out of their skin? It is rather sad to think that this is the only representation I had to refer to at the time. Thankfully, so many great representations of trans people are out there in Hollywood now. *Star Trek Discovery* have a non-binary character who uses the pronouns they/them and of course, *Orange is the New Black* had a trans woman with Laverne Cox.

However, I am not here to write about transpeople and the positive representation in Hollywood. The podcast just helped me formulate my idea for this article. Whenever I listen to Brene Brown, I am inspired to be vulnerable and share a part of my story. This part of the story is the piece of the journey of what I put my body through when I didn't understand or have the words to describe that I am non-binary. My hope is that if I can share with others this difficult part of my journey, maybe it can help others identify what that gnawing, unnamable, frustration that eats away at you when you can't seem to answer the question of "if this body doesn't feel right, what would feel right?"

When I was growing up, there wasn't a term such as non-binary. Either you were a man or you were a woman. It wasn't required that you stayed the sex you were assigned at birth. You could always change... and people did. Being transsexual or transgender wasn't unheard of when I was young, it just wasn't common place or portrayed in a very positive light as I mentioned earlier. At the time, there was a differentiation between the terms transsexual and transgender. Transsexual was defined as a person who was born as one sex then underwent surgical procedures and hormone treatment to align their body to match the opposite sex. Transgender was defined as a person whose sense of personal identity and gender does not correspond with their birth sex; however there wasn't hormone treatment or surgical intervention. Later on, transgender became the umbrella term that described those who have a different gender from the sex assigned at birth. However, there wasn't an option to be something other than a man or a woman. There wasn't the option to be something in between or neither of those two things, such as a third gender. If I didn't want to be a woman, then I would have to be a man. And I didn't want to be a man for far too many reasons. So, I was stuck, right? Maybe not.

In 2016, James Clifford Shupe became the first person in the United States to obtain legal recognition of a non-binary gender. Since then, the term non-binary has gained a lot of traction and has given a word to something people have felt, but didn't have words to describe before. Prior to that, the term genderqueer was probably the term mostly used to describe someone who didn't feel they aligned with their gender assigned at birth. This isn't to say that the idea of non-binary is new as the concept of being neither man nor woman has been shown throughout history, it just wasn't very well known. Such examples are in Native American tribes where there are more than 2 genders. Additionally, in 1776, the Public Universal Friend, born Jemima Wilkinson, identified as genderless and in 1781, Jens Andersson believed themselves to belong to both genders. But, the concept of non-binary being a third gender where one didn't have to conform to being a woman or a man, didn't take hold until very recently. I hadn't heard about it until roughly 2018 when I was visiting my friend, Pam, whose spouse was transitioning from female to male. She was telling me some of the changes her spouse was experiencing such as facial hair, fat redistribution, deepening of his voice, and muscle growth since he started HRT. My ears perked up when she mentioned fat redistribution

"Yeah, I've thought about the fat redistribution." I started to explain. "But, I don't know. I don't want to be a man, you know? I don't feel like a man. Clearly, I don't exactly feel like a woman either." I stated, gesturing to all of me.

Pam gave me a once over with my beanie, tank top, and long shorts and gave me a knowing smirk.

"Well, there's also non-binary."

"What is this magic of which you speak?" I asked.

Pam laughed and then started to explain what non-binary is and how it was being considered a third gender. I was very intrigued and was surprised at how much it resonated with me. Pam also introduced me to binders and really was the person who started me on my transgender journey. I owe a lot to her. Thanks Pam!

Once I had a word for what I had felt inside for a long time, I started to reflect back over my life and what I had been trying to achieve with my body for so long. Before I go into what exactly I mean by this, let me explain something. What I'm about to tell you is from my point of view. I am an AFAB*, non-binary person. What I am trying to achieve is my picture of what I want for my body as non-binary. That picture can vary for every non-binary person out there as non-binary people can be AFAB or AMAB (i.e.: AFAB: Assigned female at birth AMAB: Assigned male at birth) and can have different goals for themselves and their bodies. This is what my goals are for myself.

One of the first memories I have that I can identify as wishing my body was something else was in my late teenage years. I was sitting in the chow hall at the Air Force base I was assigned to and a person walked in that caught my eye. I couldn't tell if they were a man or a woman. The way their uniform sat on their hips or by the way their shirt was tucked into their pants I couldn't determine if they had feminine curves or masculine lines. When I looked at the profile of their face, their jaw line and brow could have gone either way. I

felt what I now can identify as a pang of envy. At the time, I didn't know what the feeling was I was experiencing, I just knew I was fascinated by this person. What I am certain of is how I treated my body for many years following this encounter. It wasn't specifically because of this person I saw, but because I knew something wasn't right with my body the way it was made.

What I actually thought was wrong with my body was that it was fat. We live in a society that tells us that if you are fat, you aren't attractive or you have little value. This is inherently not true. However, we are bombarded by media that show us people with very little body fat and no flaws, so we get direct and indirect messages that this is what is considered beautiful and valuable. Since I had body fat and I felt like something was wrong with my body even though I couldn't really identify what it was, I assumed it was fat. In addition to that, I also heard from my father that fat people were unattractive as well. This confirmed to me that it must be true that this uncomfortable feeling I had inside of me was that I was fat and unattractive. Neither of these thoughts were true, but because I had this undefined discomfort within in me and I had messages from several sources that said there was an "ideal" size required to be accepted, I believed these thoughts. Therefore, I would diet or work out in unhealthy and in healthy ways to try to rid myself of fat. I would lose weight, but still the uncomfortable feeling would linger. Something continued to be wrong, yet I did not have the language to define the discomfort. The war on my body continued.

The next thing I decided I was going to do was to have liposuction. This was clearly going to be the answer. I know what you must be thinking; what a drastic and costly venture to take in order to try to relieve myself of this discomfort! You would be correct. Liposuction is considered a major surgery and due to the large area I wished to have done, it had to be divided up into two separate surgeries. To define "large area" for you, I had from the top of my rib cage all the way down to my ankles done in some form or fashion. I was in a compression suit for months while I healed and was stiff and sore for a long time. I thought this had done the trick in silencing that nagging feeling within me because finally I had rid myself of the fat. But, I was wrong. Something still wasn't right. Soon, it was my chest that became my focus.

I started to want a reduction and I justified it by saying how I had always hated my breasts from the moment they started developing. I would say they are too big or they don't fit my persona being more masculine. I would wear sports bras to try to strap them down tighter than a normal bra. I just hated how much they protruded. I begged my mother to help me with the cost of a breast reduction because insurance wouldn't pay for it. I didn't have any back issues because of the size of them, they were technically normal sized breasts. But, she refused. I tried creams that were supposed to help reduce fat on the body. I tried working out and dieting again. I say again as if I ever stopped, but I changed it to be more "healthy" to try to lower my body fat. Then came a day when I started a job in a different state where my insurance covered top surgery for those who suffered from gender dysphoria. This prompted me to look into what the criteria was for gender dysphoria and that is when my journey in understanding myself began. However, I had found a solution to my chest issue!

I don't know if you are starting to notice a pattern here or not. It took me a long time to really identify it. What I came to realize after years of torturing my body was that what I was fighting was curves. It wasn't that I was actually afraid of being fat...I was afraid of having curves. I didn't want the hour glass figure of a woman I currently possessed. I wanted a flat chest with wider shoulders and narrow hips. What I was doing to my body was fighting a losing battle. I was trying to fight against the hormones in my body that told it that I was supposed to have curves with specific features. Until I understood what that nagging feeling was inside of me that kept telling my there was something wrong,I literally tortured my body with unhealthy methods of eating, working out, and the wrong surgery.

Why am I telling you this story? Because I want people to know what I did to myself until I realized that what I really wanted was a non-binary body. I want people to start questioning gender norms and the typically understood ideas of binary forms and realize that they can be what is most comfortable for them. People no longer have to be either a man or a woman when it comes to deciding their gender identity and I want to be a part of breaking that stigma apart and showing people they can embrace their own concept of non-binarism. I want people to start thinking outside the box and embrace who they want to be and be proud. I hope that my story can help some people recognize within themselves something they are feeling, but not quite able to name. That it can prevent them from having to go through what I went through. That all they have to do is shatter the societal gender construct and embrace your true authentic self.

Quinn Gathercole is a Licensed Mental Health Counselor practicing in Western Massachusetts. They have been practicing for 4 years and specialize in the LGBTQ+ community focusing on gender identity. Quinn also is skilled in trauma work and utilizes several different approaches to therapy that best suits the client's needs. Such approaches include EMDR, TF-CBT, DBT, and person centered modalities. Quinn received their Bachelor's in Psychology from the University of Central Florida and continued on to Walden University where they obtained a Masters in Mental Health Counseling and Forensic Psychology. Quinn values thinking outside the box and likes to help others realize there doesn't have to be a box to define oneself. In their personal time, Quinn enjoys outdoor activities such as kayaking and hiking as well as some down time reading a good book.

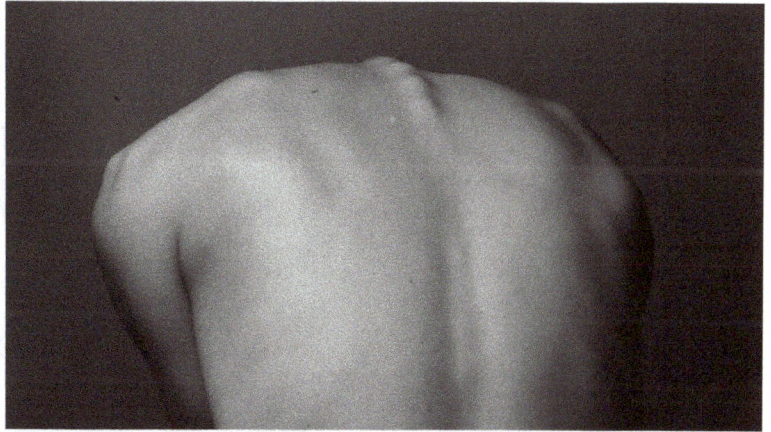

THE
COURAGE
OF DAFFODILS
BY DAVID K. LEFF

And where you see clouds upon the hills
You soon will see crowds of daffodils
"April Showers," —B. G. De Sylva

Daffodils are a sweet, cultivated obsession. By mid-April I see them everywhere in southern New England. No spring flower is more widely planted, along with their close relatives narcissi and jonquils. Long extolled by poets and artists for their beauty, it's the contagious courage of daffodils that I find most endearing.

At mid-month, my wife Mary and I often find ourselves in a sloping landscape threaded with lichen crusted stonewalls and rock outcrops where thousands of the flowers grow in clusters beneath mature sugar maples. In an area squeezed between dense woods and a cattle pasture, we've made our way down a grassy path to a pond where more flowers grow on small islands. Though we invariably arrive in the middle of a weekday, there are many other visitors making a pilgrimage to Laurel Ridge Foundation in Litchfield, Connecticut where thousands of daffodils of every description have bloomed since the early 1940s when they were planted by farsighted Remy and Virginia Morosani.

It's a peaceful sanctuary perched on the corner of wild and cultivated where elderly couples, young lovers, and parents with little children walk slowly and absorb the quiet as the flowers sway in gentle breezes. Traditional yellow daffodils and white narcissi stand out among green grasses fattened with spring rains. There are seemingly endless varieties, some with ruffled petals, orange centers, and other more subtle distinctions. They seem so bright and eager, tender looking, a living and palpable metaphor for spring. We imagine they have faces, and wonder if they speak or listen with their trumpet-like tubes surrounded by six petals forming a star-shape.

Early spring could be called daffodil season in Connecticut. They adorn home gardens and corporate landscapes. I see them planted in the formal beds of city parks like Hartford's Bushnell, and encircling civic monuments. They grow wild on hillsides beneath budding trees. Surprisingly,

I find them along roads and in ditches where they beckon with hidden stories causing me to wonder how they arrived at the pavement's edge. Occasionally I find them in deep woods where a search usually reveals a nearby house foundation, overgrown and half filled.

Native to North Africa and adjacent Western Europe, daffodils have been gardened for over 2,000 years. Testament to people's love affair with the flowers, they've been planted around the planet wherever there's suitable habitat. Human fascination with them has resulted in around 25,000 cultivars.

Something about daffodils inspires creative work. They adorn the verse of Shakespeare, Tennyson and many other poets. William Cullen Bryant called the daffodil "our doorside queen," and to nineteenth century Irishman Aubrey De Vere they were the "Love-star of the unbeloved March." William Wordsworth is famous for his verses about "a host of golden daffodils." For centuries, painters have found them irresistible subjects. "Madonna of the Daffodils with the Christ Child and Donors" (1535) by Netherlandish painter Jan van Scorel depicts a woman holding the flowers. A bright field of daffodils grow beneath trees in Vincent van Gogh's "Undergrowth with Figures" (1890), and American Charles Demuth painted an alluring watercolor bouquet entitled "Jonquils" (1928) that is so vibrant you can almost smell the blooms.

So what is it about daffodils that drives gardeners, inspires artists, and makes ordinary people stop and stare to rejoice in the season? Science educator Anna Botsford Comstock, who taught at Cornell in the early twentieth century, wrote that "they bring sunshine color to the sodden earth . . . and the sight of daffodils floods the spirit with a sense of sunlight." This is the courage to grow, to have hope.

Every spring I watch daily as my garden daffodils poke their slender, rich green leaves through half frozen ground still largely snow covered. By their growth I measure the progress of the season, slowed on cool weeks, accelerated in a warm spell. I delight in a cold spring that enables flowers to linger, the yellow ones dipped in sunshine, the white like fragments of fallen clouds.

Year after year they persist. While tulips and other flowers fade and disappear, I know that daffodils will not only return with longer and warmer days, but will thrive, thicken, and spread. Without fail they emerge, even in ancient cemeteries, beside old well curbs, along rotted fences, and at the edge of abandoned roads where nothing has been cultivated for decades. They evidence a human past, are a fragment of lost tales.

I admire the way daffodils are at home in formal gardens, but can naturalize in places that have no tending, that are not subject to shovel and rake. They adapt, become part of the landscape in a way we humans can only aspire.

Perhaps there is no location where the courage of daffodils stands in such stark relief as Meriden, Connecticut, a traditional small New England industrial city that lost its principal industries and fell on hard times. Flowers are not the first thing that comes to mind when most folks think of such a place, yet Meriden's annual Daffodil Festival on the last weekend in April has become a regional attraction, a vibrant, perfect venue for celebrating the possibilities of renewal for which daffodils are an icon.

Held in Hubbard Park with its broad lawns, mature trees, waterfall, and walkway around aptly named Mirror Lake, it's said that over 600,000 daffodils grow in orderly plantings and in semi wild clumps on tree shaded slopes near the water. The two day event features amusement rides; a village of crafters in small booths; tables and banners set up by civic organizations and businesses; multiple stages for a continuous flow of live music; and a huge food tent offering all the usual fair fare from fried dough to wings, burgers to donuts. There's a parade, fireworks, and even a Little Miss Daffodil.

My last visit was on a cool day when the flowers danced in a stiff breeze. Despite less-than-optimal weather, the festival grounds were busy with people of all ages and backgrounds strolling along the bloom lined paths, listening to music, and enjoying guilty-pleasure foods. There were lots of relaxed conversations and laughter, like you might share on vacation. Though most famous for its lost historic silver industry, it's hard not to have the courage of optimism for the future when contemplating daffodils, and hope is a great medicine for a place and its people.

Given the power of hope, it's no wonder that daffodils have become the symbol of fighting cancer. The American Cancer Society sponsors Daffodil Days mixing that hope with the beauty of flowers to raise funds. And the blooms have become more than metaphor as research reveals that a natural alkaloid extracted from daffodils has anti-cancer effects.

I hope for a cool spring and a long run for daffodils. But, by the second week in May, the flowers will be disappearing and the leaves beginning to wither and dry out. I'll miss those cheerful floral faces, but I won't be sad. I know they'll be back next year.

David K. Leff is an award-winning essayist, poet laureate of Canton, Connecticut, and former deputy commissioner of the Connecticut Department of Environmental Protection. By appointment of the National Park Service he served as poet-in-residence for the New England National Scenic Trail (NET) for 2016-17. View his work at www. davidkleff.com

GIFTS OF THE ORDINARY

THE MINDFUL KITCHEN BY HEIDI BARR

At a glance, most days of the average human being are rather unremarkable. As the sun starts to think about showing up for the day at my house, we put the coffee on and eat breakfast. Everyone scrambles to get dressed, and then we're off and running toward whatever is on the agenda. Work, school, errands. Dishes need to be done, the cat box needs cleaning, someone has a dentist appointment. The mundane to-do lists of a home or office weekday hang out in the corner, quietly demanding attention. Unremarkable.

Yet at second glance, on a seemingly ordinary day, somewhere in the world the snow sparkles just so in the sun. Fog softens a rough edge. A newborn cries. An elder starts to fade. An old oak tree falls to the ground to see what it's like to practice resurrection in the form of decay and rebirth. Minutes pass, days are lived, months stack themselves up. Every year that ticks by reminds me how much being alive changes with the passing of time and how an understanding of time shifts with age. The days are long, but the years are short. Maybe this cliché is true. Maybe we just learn to see another layer of experience when caring for others, or when we are being cared for. Maybe how we walk through time shifts with every step we take further into our arc of life. I don't know. What I do know is that an unremarkable day can be full of wonder if we pay attention. Witnessing part of another life taking shape shapes us. Any day has the potential to serve as a poignant reminder that being alive and in community with other living things is anything but unremarkable. Any day has the potential to remind us that something like God might just be in our midst, despite everything.

Life is happening all around us, starting and stopping and starting again in ways we don't always understand. Every day we have a chance to celebrate the fact that we are on the planet at this exact moment in time. We are here, now, sharing space with other beings, some who we adore and some who we do not, some who we see clearly and some who need to be seen much more than they are. We have the opportunity to truly see them and to truly see ourselves. We can choose to view the passing of minutes, days, and years as gifts instead of something to resign ourselves to or dread. We have the opportunity to see astonishments in the mundane and blessings in the ordinary.

Speaking of gifts of the ordinary, here's a recipe to celebrate simple spring blessings. *excerpted from *Slouching Toward Radiance*

Creamy Asparagus Penne

1 lb whole wheat penne

½ lb steamed asparagus

1 cup whole milk

2 tablespoons butter

1 tablespoon flour

½ cup parmesan cheese, grated

Salt and pepper to taste

Melt butter in a heavy bottomed saucepan. Whisk in the flour to make a roux, then gradually whisk in milk. Stir continuously until thickened and add grated cheese, continuing to stir until the cheese is melted. Meanwhile, cook pasta according to its package's instructions. Add pasta and steamed asparagus to cheese sauce and mix til combined. Serve immediately, adding salt and pepper to taste and more cheese if desired. Serves 4.

Award winning author of several books, Heidi Barr is committed to cultivating ways of being that are life-giving and sustainable for people, communities and the planet. She works as a wellness coach, holds a Master's degree in Faith and Health Ministries and occasionally partners with organic farms and yoga teachers to offer retreat experiences. At home in Minnesota, she lives with her husband and daughter where they tend a large vegetable garden, explore nature and do their best to live simply. Visit her at www.heidibarr.com

POETRY

"Poetry is the lifeblood of rebellion, revolution,
and the raising of consciousness."
—Alice Walker

WILL FALK
FEATURED POET

———

ANTHROPOCENE WRITER'S BLOCK

(for the trees)

Sometimes when I sit down to write,
visions rise from the paper.

Desperate men come for me.
Sometimes, they crack my head open
to see what's inside.
Other times, it's a slow parts-per-million poison,
that they're sorry,
but, let me assure you,
they never knew was harmful.
The best times are the quick, painless injections
that leave no mark
and don't affect my market value.

They turn my skin into leather,
and design exotic shoes for expensive parties.
They stretch me across cushions,
take afternoon naps, and always ignore their dreams.

They line their jacket hoods with my hair,
which keeps wind from whispering in their ear,
keeps winter from touching
cozy hearts in sheltered chests.

One of them, especially creative,
builds a xylophone with my bones
and plays the dirtiest,
the funkiest,
the sickest beats, ever
for the ones tapping their toes
in my skin shoes.

It's hard to blame them.
They're just creating beauty, after all,
And, if not beauty,
they're just doing their jobs.
There's rent, other bills,
food on the table,
and we all gotta eat,

don't we?

When the xylophone fades away,
and the couch is finally refurbished,
I see the murdered tree
in the paper in front of me.
My burning skin and sore bones
wonder what chemical scribbles
I can tattoo on this tree's flesh
that would bring the tree
back to life,
so she could forgive me.

THIS AMERICAN SOLSTICE

Light, made stronger by the dark,
flows from the half moon,
and makes the long journey down
to dance with her bright kin, the flames
leaping from a thousand bonfires.

Druid whispers are almost audible
as they scatter from groves of ancient, murdered oak.
The whispers ride coffin ships and railroad cars
to diasporize across oceans and a continent
seeking the children of those
they once taught to understand.

Now, only the shadows comprehend.

And, where the shadows flicker,
stag heads shift into wolves
singing to the stars.
Stars gather into flapping eagle wings
descending into salmon tails
churning cold, emerald streams.
Streams swirl around strong trees
rooted in the land that creates all of this.

But, it's a different darkness, here,
on this American solstice.
The stories are difficult to recognize.
We are generations
and too many forgotten languages from home.

A DYING TRICKSTER'S LAST JOKE

A dying, mangy coyote ran along I-70
across the cold, Colorado prairie.

As fast as he was, he wasn't fast enough
to outrun the tiny mites stripping him naked
or to catch a little heat from each falling star.

When the stars burned out,
as he knew they always do,
he turned towards the highway
seeking the warm, diesel exhaust
the trucks leave in their wake.

He might have been looking for one last joke –
the kind he and his trickster kin have always played.

But, it must not have been funny enough
that an animal who had dodged
rifle-shots, semi-trucks, and cyanide
would finally die
because rodenticides meant for rats and mice
had so weakened his immune system
he could not fight off invisible mites.

At last, he got too close to the road.
A truck swerved. And, there was a crash.

That's where I saw this freezing coyote,
trembling and shivering, licking himself,
as he gathered his few remaining tufts of fur,
and wore them like a stained and shredded sweatshirt
he pulled off someone who did not survive the wreck.

NEARLY-BLIND RUST BELT BLUES

No one warned me that the smokestacks,
skyscraper guts, and starless nights
could turn my gaze so steely.

Carp leapt from green water
to smack the flanks of coal barges
hauling the corpses of ancient ones
who never asked to be cremated.

The river carried iron and irony
to the gulf. Never before had water
been forced to participate so completely
in fueling an inferno.

It happened as slow as oxidation
until I was as rigid as a machine.
My vision frozen on things
no one was meant to see.

A great blue heron wrenched my gears.
With a flash of feathers,
she swung low,
dumped sugar into my gas tank,
and led me back to the river's
curls and curves.

I stood haunted by
all I now could see.
If it had lasted any longer
I might have had to wirebrush
the rust from my own eyes.

VIRAL POETRY

Sometimes Life speaks through poets.
Sometimes Life speaks through dreams,
through flowing water,
through chilly stars on a clear winter night,
through the imperfect reconstruction of experience
our memories strive so hard to provide,
through those moments when your loving body
knows no separation from your lover's body.

Sometimes Life speaks through pain,
through injury, illness, and epidemics.
She whispers. She shouts. She screams.
And, sometimes,
she even kills people—lots of people—
in the hopes her message is heard.

Sometimes Life speaks through viruses.
But, she would rather speak through poets.

Will Falk is an author, activist, and attorney. His first book *How Dams Fall*, a work of lyrical creative nonfiction examining his relationship with the Colorado River while representing her in the first-ever federal lawsuit seeking rights for a major ecosystem, was published in 2019 by Homebound Publications.

GWENDOLYN MORGAN

—

FLIGHT FEATHERS

We found a large flight feather
watched Red-tailed Hawk on a thermal lift
when it started to rain, we remembered.

The mother told us they put an ankle bracelet
on her when they separated her
from her children at the border crossing.

This is the same bracelets our government
uses to track prisoners, electronic surveillance
a way to monitor movement of undocumented.

The mother shared that ICE kept her two children in cages for months
"They treated us like animals," she wrote in her notebook,
"as they confirmed my identity with facial recognition."

We confirmed the identification of the hawk
with Feather Atlas, a field guide to feathers
from the Forensics Laboratory of the U.S. Fish and Wildlife Service.

SHE (WHO) SPEAKS RIVER LANGUAGE

the vocation of water is fluidity
before she tells herself
where she will flow
she (who) is already on her way to the sea.
Listen! Song of Ouzel, rock-hewn gorge,
river-stone, White-tailed Deer, Wandering Shrew
petroglyph, alder, hemlock, fir
mossy banks and branches
smell of dinghy and kayak.

She memorizes the dialect of molecular structure,
and re-members the clay bottom, the subtext.
She never forgets who she is,
or where.

Gwendolyn Morgan is a Pacific Northwest poet and artist who has served in interfaith spiritual care in medical centers and hospice for nearly two decades. She learned the names of birds and inherited horsehair paint brushes and wooden paint boxes from her grandmothers.   She was most recently a recipient of a Centrum Artist Residency. The Clark County Poet Laureate 2018-2020 in Washington State, her fourth book of poetry, *Flight Feathers*, was released by Wayfarer Books in April 2022.   As a multiracial family in a multispecies watershed, they are committed to equity work and inclusion for all.

ALAN ABRAMS

―――

THE CARELESS PERFECTION OF NATURE

(In Five Parts)

1. GRAVITY

Buzzards amuse me:
So ugly, at least to my eye,
it's a wonder they reproduce.
Yet these creatures that feed on death
are plentifully alive. Sometimes, scads of them aloft.

It's how they soar that really gets me, though—
how they rock on the axis of their flight,
wings tipping up and down—
like the arms of a drunk, struggling to walk
a sidewalk seam before a suspicious cop.

All this, in effortless defiance of gravity-
that ever-present, omnipotent force
that gives us jowls and causes our
breasts and buttocks to sag-and at
time's end, draws us down into the earth.

Yes, gaze at them and marvel-there's
likely one in view this very moment.
Then stand up, and take a walk;
and make your own rebellion against
gravity's primal field-and be alive.

2. WEEPING WILLOW

Naked and alone,
in a field not far from the creek
stands a huge weeping willow
that has not leafed out in several years.
It would not surprise me if we are the same age.
I remember it in its glory, because
I would gauge the wind-its direction, its speed-
by the flutter of its long green tendrils:
information valuable to the cyclist.
Now, others value it more;
the sapsucker, the downy, the redbelly—
and the worms they seek.
Me, I wonder why it died-
this tree that had the sun all to itself,
and plenty of water for its roots. Perhaps
it's climate change. I too have had times of drought
and infestation, miserable heat and bitter cold.
But unlike this dead willow, I am still impatient for spring.
Even so, you know where to scatter my ashes.

3. MY SPANISH IS NO GOOD

The shifting breezes barely stir the sodden flags;
the tide turns, to inch back toward the sea,
spilling yonder poplars upside down.
Redwing blackbirds scritch;
a distant dopplered airhorn makes a crossing—
and from my spokes, a whisper...

…above all this floats something sonorous—
syllables, from a man, seated on the bank--
swarthy, stubbled,
hatted, hoodied,
hands flailing, grasping air,
like the gulls beyond his reach.

My Spanish is no good,
but did I catch some words?
"Madre de Dios," or maybe not…

Who else was there, to prove my ears were wrong?
Who else, besides the black robed cormorant?
Who else, besides the sharp toed osprey?
Who else, besides the silent river?

4. EVENING IN LOS LUCEROS

Like clockwork-a little after sundown-Rosa
raises her snout from her front paws.
It's that damn skunk again. She whines and snivels
and parades back and forth until you have to open the door.
You pray that she won't find it, but you know she will.
And by the way, tomato juice does not work. Later,
after you're between the sheets, you hear the first howl.
Usually it starts up the valley, and progresses downstream
as the conversation is taken up by other coyotes,
and probably some dogs as well.
There are feral dogs, too, back in the barrancas, perhaps
abandoned as puppies, so skinny they can hardly stand.
Finally the coyotes are silent—as silent as the shooting stars.
You don't need to hear them to know they're there.

5. THE CARELESS PERFECTION OF NATURE

Damn fool oaks!
Don't they know that lightning seeks the tallest trunks?
And how about those prissy hemlocks-
so neat and frilly, so fussy in their form-
now ravaged by some hungry little worm.
Whole forests of them, denuded.
Even monstrous boulders, silent and impassive-
the ones outlasting mountains—
surrender to shape-shifting waters,

Alan Abrams is a retired architect-builder who now has more time for scribbling. He has written features for the local newspaper, and articles and reviews for professional journals. His work has appeared in *The Black Boot*, *The Innisfree Journal of Poetry*, *The Hare's Paw* and others. A novel is also in the works.

HEIDI BARR

LIFE ON EARTH

We—you and I; them and us—
we're like a great web,

spider silk stretching out
beyond horizons

Aspen roots intertwined
binding us together

clouds of misty fog
permeating our cells over here

and theirs over there.
In some ways we live apart, yet

we remain connected
through space and across time

all generations and species
colors and creeds

different parts yet one body
of blood and bone, soil and sky.

THIN PLACES

I was thinking today
about words that come alive
on your tongue, an embodied host;
about beauty that evaporates
when touched, so keep reaching;
about seekers reading poetry,
finding prayer in the lines—
about breath air life art
jumbled up vibrations,
humanity meeting itself
in the space between.

Heidi Barr lives in Minnesota with her husband and daughter, where they tend to a large vegetable garden, explore nature and do their best to live simply. She works as a wellness coach, holds a master's degree in Faith and Health Ministries, and is a 2022 Poet of Place in the lower St. Croix Valley. Author of several books of nonfiction, she is committed to cultivating ways of being that are life-giving and sustainable for people, communities, and the planet. Her latest poetry collection, *Slouching Toward Radiance*, was released in April 2022 from Homebound Publications.

GUNILLA NORRIS

WHEN YOU GET TO BE OLD

losses are the way of things.
They are like scattered treasures
abandoned on the long trek
out West seeking your fortune.

The family silver, too heavy for the wagon
is set by the rise of a steep hill, and the bureau
with your soft feminine dreams and silks
will be left by a stream, drawers open to rain.

You get the weathered boards of the wagon
instead, with the wheels under it rumbling
along for years, tipping this way and that.
You get nights full of stars and strangeness.

You get the far country where you won't
know anyone and where many things live
that you'll never care to know. Why not
make camp in the living room? Why not

arrive where you already are? It is as good
a place as any to find what remains . . .
a small stack of kindling, flint, split wood,
the smell of smoke and the moist steam

from your kettle with its humble dings
shining in moonlight and on you, too,
as you crawl out of the worn wagon
to make camp and be here as it is.

ON THE VERGE

On a day too warm for anything but shallow breathing,
a hawk came on broad brown wings, underbelly flashing
white light and landing on the verge by the sea
a spare yard away from me.

It picked at the weedy grass, ripped apart and ate a mole,
ignored me in my blue plastic chair. It fluffed its tail feathers
as if to dismiss me, a quick gesture flinging off anything
that might be in its way.

The head swivelled and it stared at me, creature to creature.
I wondered if it knew how it caused my heart to flutter
as the summer heat grew thick around me and my chair,
there on the verge.

It took its time feeding steadily. I watched as if my life
depended on it, felt its strong heart beat when it rose,
skimming over dry grass. I flicked everything off that was
in the way of rising like that.

Gunilla Norris lives in Rhode Island. She has published
three poetry books. *Joy is the Thinnest Layer* won the
Nautilus Gold Medal in 2017. Currently she is working on her
fourth book, *Old and Singing*. Though older poets are often
marginalized, she feels they should be heard for despite
their years they are packed with passion and love of life.

WALKER ABEL

—

DEER HOOF, RIVER COBBLES

She said that people once
danced with anklets of deer hoof
that out on river terrace even now
their steps pool up with moonlight.

Behind every tree, she said
an unseen column of space.
That after sticks are gathered
beauty burns with fugitive heat.

Then autumn, and he remembers again
the formations of geese, their calls
first faint, but finally high up
the flicker of light off wings.

It seemed the breath of her being
was like that, a migration
he might step into, be lost with
above geese, above clouds

fallen in with a herd of stars
traipsing the dark turf
that undergirds galaxies
exhaled into the endless hollows

before alighting again
alone, moonlit, a deer hoof
dancing on river cobbles.

THE UNCHANGING

It was then as though the world
were made of light
how it flared
in white spray of waves over rock
burned even in the blue of water
while sky burned blue as well

but lighter, as though thinned with itself
and spread so broadly as to be dimensionless
made to merge with the transparent light
that held still in its own being

not moved by forceful wind
not blocked by clouds or wings of gull
a light undiminished, full and present
in even the darkest shadow

here beneath the willows
ruffling along riverside.

Walker Abel has published four volumes of poetry, all with Homebound Publications. He lives with the weight that because of human impact, the beauty of the earth seems to be diminishing, and that nature poetry, though still celebration, also contains tones of elegy.

APRIL TIERNEY

FIELD GUIDES FOR LIBERATION

Today, in Burma, there are poets
being killed and imprisoned.

Read that sentence again.

I have read it several times
and still it barely sinks in.

What is so threatening
about the poet?

To any society bent on control
and greed, surely artists represent
the most untamable breed,

but poets wield language
as an alchemical force;

words and stories that get lodged
in our imaginations, quietly crafting
field guides for our liberation.

Maung Yu Py faces two years in prison
after being severely beaten for his poetry.
I have read the English translation
of his piece Under The Great Ice Sheet,
and it is pure beauty latched to the breast of truth.
It's something I wish every beating heart
could read or hear spoken aloud
with the dawning sun.

In my early twenties I spent some time in Thailand
and while there lent a hand at a school for Burmese refugees;
they wanted someone to teach the children English.
I knew nothing of Burmese (not to mention,
very little of English) even so, my answer was yes.

We huddled together in a one-room, makeshift schoolhouse
with brightly painted walls--sitting on the floor and sweating
in that humid, December air. There were never enough pencils
to go around, but still, we spent our days in the company

of wonder and words.
The children were all ages;
peering at me behind poets' eyes.

I have read about another Burmese writer
who spent six years in solitary confinement,
and when she was released, she kept on writing.

Today, I write alongside them.

April Tierney is a poet, craftswoman, mother, and lover of stories. She is the author of three full length collections of poetry, as well as the co-author of a chapbook and photographic anthology. This piece is from her newest collection, *Memory Keeper*, published in April 2022 by Wayfarer Books. She lives in the hills above Lyons with her husband, young daughter, mischievous dog, and wide web of kin. To learn more visit www.apriltierney.com.

L.M. BROWNING

THIS IS WHAT YOU SHALL DO *AND NOT DO*

Know your worth, know your limits, know your boundlessness, know your strengths, know your weaknesses, know your accomplishments, and know your dreams.

Be a mirror for all those who project their darkness onto you; do not internalize it. Don't seek validation from those who will refuse to understand you. Don't say yes, when you need to say no. Don't stay when you know you should go. Don't go when you know you should stay. Respond, don't react. Behave in a manner aligning with your values.

Sleep. Seek out quiet. Don't glorify busyness. Reignite your curiosity for the world. Explore new horizons. Be honest with yourself. Be gentle with yourself. Approach yourself as you would approach a child—with a kind tone and deep understanding. Love yourself or, at the very least, have mercy on yourself. Be your own parent, your own child, your own lover, your own partner.

Give less of your time to employment that drains you of your enthusiasm for life. Reclaim your freedom by redefining your necessities. Take that gathered energy; devote your precious life to your passions.

Unplug from the babble. Seek awe. It is the counterbalance to trauma. Do your psychological work, and don't take any one else's work upon yourself. Protect your peace. Listen to what your heart knows; *fuck* everything else.

WHEN IT IS FIXIN' TO STORM

Go now. Go West
—go toward yourself.

Take that freedom and ride it to the coast
—until it breaks down or builds up.

Wear those old boots again
—the ones that peeled apart at the sole
            only to be remade.

Let the grief burn
—let it hollow you out

Just let it be what it was
    —sit with it,
    hear it,
    feel it,
    follow it,
    then listen.

... drive through the night, darlin'.
The only way home,
is through.

L.M. Browning (she/them) is a TEDx speaker, award-winning author, and mountain homesteader. In her writing, Browning explores the confluence of the natural landscape and the interior landscape. She lives deep in the Berkshires of Massachusetts. When not writing or publishing the work of indie authors, she is roaming the mountains . . . which are ever-calling.

FRANK INZAN OWEN

———

SHUGENJA HILLWALKER'S ANTHEM

Feet tired.

Face burned by the sun.

I wouldn't have it any other way!

Uketamo!

Flowing with mountains.

Bathing in the honeysuckle wind.

I wouldn't have it any other way!

Uketamo!

Uketamo!

———

*uketamo is a Japanese word that encapsulates a particular philosophy among certain yamabushi monks, hermits, and lay people. A loose translation is: "I accept."

DESPITE CLOUD COVER

The light of the moon
is transmitting new teachings
despite cloud cover.

A DAY TO UNFURL THE MIND

Swaying pines.

Clouds rolling in.

Heart-Mind stirs.

A thought-bubble floats by:

"What might it be like

to have a nation guided

not by Mao,

not by Dow,

but Dao?"

WHAT DOES IT MEAN
TO BE A PERSON OF THE WAY?

Pledge allegiance
to remaining aware
of the precious world
that passes from form
not the one that grasps and grasps
and tries to hold on.

Frank Inzan Owen (隱山, Hidden Mountain) is a poet, gardener, hillwalker, and Wayfarer of a Nature-oriented spiritual path shaped by Daoist and Japanese spiritual principles. In addition to penning three books of poetry on Homebound Publications, he is a facilitator of contemplative soulwork through his organization the School of Soft-Attention (schoolofsoftattention.com).

QUINN BAILEY

HEALING

It will come unannounced
and unwelcome at first,
a swelling in the chest,
a moth in your throat that
refuses to be swallowed,
until you are down on
your hands and knees,
in the rosy-gray light
of the pasture,
the thistles catching
silvery strings of mucus
stretching down
to the muddy ground,
as sobs for a childhood
that could have been yours
send the ducks flapping
furiously up off the pond,
and a secret part of you
slumps with relief like
an old skiff finally surrendered
to the hungry waves.

Quinn Bailey is a poet, naturalist, and wildlife tracker who
writes from his strong sense of belonging and curiosity about
the natural world. He feels most at home wandering the wooded
hills and rocky shores surrounding the Salish Sea where he was
born and raised. Quinn's work has appeared in publications
such as *Sharks Reef, Deep Wild*, and *Big Sky Journal*. His first
full-length collection of poetry, *The Currents of the World*
(Homebound 2020), is available wherever books are sold.
Learn more at quinnbailey.com.

I DON'T BELIEVE IN GOD

not as any sort of
person shaped thing
anyway. But if I did
I would imagine them
as an amateur painter,
constantly at work on
their masterpiece—

The sky

hat slightly askew,
their frock stiff with an
eternity of mistakes
and spilled paint,
trying, once again,
to get the pink clouds
just right.

MY MOTHERS DREAM

The tiger eats you,
And you feel nothing

But ecstasy. Swallowing
Your broken form into her

Red blood growing the lush fields
Of orange, and black, and white

No fear, just quiet elation as
Your muscle becomes

Muscle in service
To a better beast.

ROBERT BRODER

—

ADIRONDACK CHAIRS

Mom
if i could be with you
for a day
we'd sit by the lake
Adirondack chairs
good coffee
good chocolate
and talk
i would hold your hand
my skin is now older than yours
feeling your soft fingers
i'd tell you
the person I have become
even if you already know
the sadness, pain,
and anger
i have endured
from losing Stella
and how the mourning
was long and difficult
I would try and make you laugh
with my sarcastic sense of humor

and share my travels with Nathan
showing you his paw print
tattooed on my ankle
how walking in the woods alone is my favorite thing
i'd want to hear about your childhood,
because i was too young to ask
about losing your dad
meeting daddy
and starting a life together
in the last few hours of the day
as the sun sets
behind the Adirondack Mountains
I would want you to meet Eleanor Moon
to play, be silly,
and to see how wonderful she is
for her to meet you
to see your beautiful you
to hear your sweet voice
one last time
before we say
goodbye.

Robert Broder is a children's book author and founding publisher of award-winning Ripple Grove Press. He is the writer of Patagonia's first picture book titled *Better Than New*. Other books include *Crow & Snow* (Simon and Schuster) and *Our Shed* (Little Bigfoot) which received a Kirkus Starred Review. He enjoys walking in the snow, running at the farm, hiking in the woods, and drinking coffee on the couch. He lives with his family in a small town, near a big lake, surrounded by green mountains. He is Poet Laureate of Shelburne, Vermont. See more at RobertBroder.com

RICK BENJAMIN

―

CREDO
after Alicia Hokanson

I believe in early-morning
dolphins feeding on crill
at the wave-line,

in oatmeal, hot, in early
spring, I believe

in quiet talk first thing
before the day's

turned to the many
wars, to the people

now living without
ceilings, doors, & to

the people already
living without them,

in hearts that reach
toward any seed or

root worth growing
& I believe in that

knowing that comes
with the fruit

of your labor, in
what even a tongue

can savor, &, often,
does. I believe

in this morning
waking up, same

as always near you,
in our spoon-to-

spoon clinging
gently to this life

without needing
too much from it

& in gratitude,
in gratitude.

Rick Benjamin lives on Chumash land in Goleta, California, and walks each day on indigenous trails. He teaches courses at the University of California Santa Barbara, among them poetry and community, wild literature, reimagining social change, & juvenile justice, while also working among elders, young people at a local Boys and Girls Club, in art museums and youth detention facilities. Among his works are the books of poetry, Passing Love, Floating World, Endless Distances, and Some Bodies in the Grief Bed. He served as the poet laureate of Rhode Island from 2012 – 2016.

AMY NAWROCKI

KILLING DARLINGS

Unfill the water glass, unfinish the letter,
unopen the window. Unsee
the unfed birds in their feeder of unclaimed space.
The great negative of the unfathomable.
Everybody's got something
worth killing.

There are some unsorted out thoughts
about acorns and un-oak trees. There is also
an undefined black wing, an unfinished worm,
a laurel branch secured in the unrecognizable
vision of my unaided eyes. At a loss now,
as imprecise as my darling *un*. I cannot kill you.

Everybody's got something, and today
I have a garden of acorns, unplanted
in the cracked blacktop, a rookery
of squawks and unmistakable crows who
undecorate the stillness with chatter
and unmusical melodies. Everything
has something. Every body has a small piece
of an uneaten morsel, the uncluttered space
between quiet and sound, between expected
and unrecognized, the darlings of unkilled thoughts.

Everybody's got something, and I have
unperfect and unlovely,
everything unspoken.

PORTAL

Light through sheer clouds
lays in green-tinted tracing paper
an opening, an awning of likeliness.

Once day comes into itself,
the likeness will buzz
with lobed sassafras and birch bark
beginning to fray.

ANTE MERIDIEM

The mainframe still thinks it's night.
A half moon, yellow and curved like a fingernail,
tells me a false temperature: yesterday's nightshade
warmed the sky less than this morning's burning orb.
There are no rain drops in last night's forecast.
No crickets to report on, no slumber time stamped.

By the time I've made this note in my head,
the algorithms have found their calculations
and have settled on seventy-two degrees, half sun
half puffy cloud-like portraits of clouds.
The day is in its seventh hour,
old enough to hold bones and bite blue.

www.ingramcontent.com/pod-product-compliance
Lightning Source LLC
Chambersburg PA
CBHW081035050426
42335CB00053B/2822